Printed in Great Britain
by Amazon

32486055R00115